Maggi from Charles 1975

THE MIDNIGHT SKATERS

EDMUND BLUNDEN

The Midnight Skaters

*Poems for young readers chosen
and introduced
by*

C. Day Lewis

ILLUSTRATIONS BY
David Gentleman

THE BODLEY HEAD
LONDON SYDNEY
TORONTO

This collection © Edmund Blunden 1968
Foreword © The Bodley Head Ltd 1968
Illustrations © The Bodley Head Ltd 1968
Printed and bound in Great Britain for
The Bodley Head Ltd
9 Bow Street, London WC2
by William Clowes & Sons Ltd, Beccles
Set in Monotype Baskerville
This collection first published 1968

Introduction by

C. DAY LEWIS

Edmund Blunden, when last I saw him, seemed to have changed little in manner or feature from the man I had first met at Oxford well over thirty years ago. The impression he gives is still one of interestedness, alertness, inner liveliness. In conversation, he tilts his head sideways, looking down— the attitude of a thrush listening for worms beneath a lawn. He is small, birdlike, beaky (so many good poets have had a prominent bridge to their noses).

He has been called a 'pastoral poet', which irritates him a good deal: for, though many of his poems come out of the English countryside—particularly Kent, where he was born —his experience and enthusiasms have ranged much wider. They include the 1914 war: he was pitched into the Western Front while still almost a boy, and survived to win the M.C. and write one of the finest books about that conflict, *Undertones of War*. He has spent long periods in the Far East, teaching literature in the University of Tokyo and Hong Kong University, winning thousands of oriental students to his subject and himself. He has accomplished much in criticism, reviving our interest in the poetry of Clare, writing studies of Vaughan, Shelley, Keats, Coleridge, Hardy, and editing the poems of Collins, Smart, Wilfred Owen, Ivor Gurney. He was a keen batsman and wicket-keeper. In 1966, the year of his seventieth birthday, he was honoured by election to the Oxford Chair of Poetry, and his birthday celebrations produced tributes from people all over the world—being so modest a man, he may well not have realised till then what a host of friends and admirers he has.

When we are young, if we like poetry at all we are drawn to that of the great masters or that of our near-contemporaries. There are fashions in poetry, as in everything else. An old poet, still writing, is likely to be out of fashion with people forty or fifty years younger. Blunden has never been fashionable, as Eliot, say, or Betjeman, or the Beat poets have been. To say this is not to run down the one or the others. All it means is that Blunden has not swept readers off their feet by originality, by technical daring, or by any kind of eccentricity. He has worked quietly away, in one of the central English traditions, giving to it his own thoughtfulness, love of nature, moods of joy and melancholy, his own strains of gentleness and toughness.

Toughness and gentleness seem to be at the core of the English character. In this respect, Blunden is pre-eminently an *English* poet. A merely gentle poem is likely to be an insipid one: a poem which relies too much on toughness may in the course of time end up by sounding merely aggressive. In his best work, Blunden balances these two qualities against each other—a gentle ruminating cast of mind using words in a way that is precise and hard.

Look at 'The Child's Grave' (p. 45). The poet is visiting the grave of his daughter, Joy, who died very young. How difficult not to write a sentimental poem about this! But it is, in every sense, a joy-full one: death is an unanswered riddle, but grief has been lived through, and it is spring again. Or take one of Blunden's best-known poems, 'The Midnight Skaters' (p. 92). Death awaits us under the ice—and it is very thin ice: but 'Court him, elude him, reel and pass, And let him hate you through the glass'. The exhilaration of danger, like the exhilaration of spring in 'The Child's Grave', subdues the presence of death. But in neither poem is the fact of death shirked: Blunden is an honest poet.

Another famous poem of his, 'Forefathers' (p. 18), gives us the same delight in simply being alive. The poet thinks back over the continuity of village life, generation replacing generation—the poem has much in common with Gray's Elegy: he pays tribute to the virtues of his ancestors, the rude forefathers of the hamlet, in spare, brisk words; but the last stanza, with its lyrical second and third lines, makes clear his intoxication with the living present.

Piety, which to the old Romans meant, among other things, a reverence for one's roots and for the past, is a strong element in Blunden's verse. You find it in 'Forefathers', and —very differently expressed—in 'Farm Bailiff' (p. 20). The man he lovingly describes here has been a part of his own boyhood as well as of the village life. We are lucky if, when we are young, we get to know some older person who seems to us larger than life—a hero figure who makes the world more enchanting for us, rouses our emulation and sharpens our appetite for living. And for loving. Blunden has a great feeling for friendship: you can hear it in 'Almswomen' (p. 22), where two old women in a village almshouse, lifelong friends, have grown so close that their only wish is for both of them (and their pet bird) to die together on the same day.

It is the value of friendship, together with the ruin man made of nature, which comes most powerfully out of Blunden's war poems. Because the natural scene was so near to his heart, he sometimes seems almost as outraged by what shell-fire did to the French countryside as by its wholesale destruction of men. The front-line soldiers of the 1914 war had little left them but comradeship and its rough humour: they did not hate the enemy soldiers, who were living in the same hell as themselves: they had to learn a fatalistic acceptance of dying, and try to face death 'with that one hope, disdain', as we read in 'The Zonnebeke Road' (p. 50). For the young poet, the danger was that the inferno he lived in would prove so shattering an experience that, even if he survived, the springs of poetry would have dried up in him.

Blunden escaped both these fates. But for many years after it he harked back in poems to episodes of the war. He has never quite succeeded in exorcising its millions of ghosts. And one result of this was to make *him* feel a ghost, as his dead friends were, among the living. The delayed reaction is described in what I think is the finest of his war poems, '1916 Seen from 1921' (p. 59):

> . . . and I
> Dead as the men I loved, wait while life drags
> Its wounded length from those sad streets of war
> Into green places here, that were my own;
> But now what once was mine is mine no more,
> I seek such neighbours here and I find none.

Such moods of utter desolation are rare in Blunden's poetry. They can be matched with moods, no less rare, of a wider disillusionment. You find it in the first three stanzas of 'Report on Experience' (p. 94): here, the sombre findings of his Report are touched by a kind of savage levity; and in the last stanza he declares (do you believe him?) that 'These disillusions are His curious proving That He loves humanity'. Another poem I particularly like, so clear on the surface, so riddling beneath it, is 'The Sunlit Vale' (p. 93). Just what *is* going on here? Is he taking a swipe at 'the pastoral fairy-tale', the deceptive charm of nature? Who is 'that other' who 'does not smile'? Death? God?

Turn back to the nature poems. For most of us today the country is a holiday place, like the seaside. But Blunden was born and bred there, at a time when country children had fewer and simpler amusements than most young people have today: no cinema, radio, telly, pop records, elaborate toys. They made do with what lay close to hand. It was a narrower life, but one which went deeper. You learned nature by heart, rather than studying botany, ornithology etc. As a sensitive boy, Blunden absorbed into his bloodstream the seasons, the neighbours, the birds, fish, animals, flowers: as an observant one, he consciously noted their detail: when he had grown up, he found the gift of words to describe such things accurately and with the familiarity of the insider.

Other poets, particularly in our own time, have tried to do for city life what poetry through many centuries has done for the country life—make its sights, sounds, manners, character the material of their art. When we think of 'modern poetry', we tend to think of town-based poetry. But this must not mean that we should look on the country poet as out of date, or his work as out of key with our modern way of living. Our most impressionable years are those of our youth, and it is from the experience of those years that a poet collects the memories which are the main source of his poetry. Blunden's most impressionable years were spent in the country and on the Western Front, and it is natural that the bulk of his verse should reflect those early experiences.

The best of his country poems, though some of them may be a bit bookish, are never tame. Just as amid the terrors and comradeship of the war he does not lose sight of nature, so in his country poems we are made aware of nature's cruelty as well as its beauty. A note of disquiet, or of harshness, can be heard in them sometimes: and always there is that air of attentiveness.

This selection opens with a large group of poems I have called 'Country Things and People'. The range is wide, from a blue butterfly to a killer pike, from a mole-catcher to a poor man's pig, from gipsies to a village schoolmaster, from a may-day lyric to the pathos of a country sale. A sense of the

11

seasons and the changeful weather of the human heart runs through them all. The same tenderness and toughness are there in the next section, 'War Remembered'. I have followed this with groups of poems about China and Japan, and about some of the poets—Clare, Shelley, Hardy—for whom Blunden has a special affection. At the end I have put a section called 'Mysteries'. I do not mean that these set out to be puzzle poems, though one or two of them are pretty enigmatic to me. But all of them, in their varying ways, give you the impression of having more in them than meets the eye. They set a scene, but then the scene shifts, and you find yourself in unfamiliar country; or they start at a certain level, but then drop you unexpectedly to a profounder one. They point to depths, which you must explore and ponder for yourself.

C. DAY LEWIS

Contents

MYSTERIES (*contd.*)

COUNTRY THINGS
AND PEOPLE

FOREFATHERS

Here they went with smock and crook,
  Toiled in the sun, lolled in the shade,
Here they mudded out the brook
  And here their hatchet cleared the glade:
Harvest-supper woke their wit,
Huntsman's moon their wooings lit.

From this church they led their brides,
  From this church themselves were led
Shoulder-high; on these waysides
  Sat to take their beer and bread.
Names are gone—what men they were
These their cottages declare.

Names are vanished, save the few
  In the old brown Bible scrawled;
These were men of pith and thew,
  Whom the city never called;
Scarce could read or hold a quill,
Built the barn, the forge, the mill.

On the green they watched their sons
  Playing till too dark to see,
As their fathers watched them once,
  As my father once watched me;
While the bat and beetle flew
On the warm air webbed with dew.

Unrecorded, unrenowned,
   Men from whom my ways begin,
Here I know you by your ground
   But I know you not within—
There is silence, there survives
Not a moment of your lives.

Like the bee that now is blown
   Honey-heavy on my hand,
From his toppling tansy-throne
   In the green tempestuous land—
I'm in clover now, nor know
Who made honey long ago.

FARM BAILIFF

PART II

Old Albert—Father Cheeseman,—so all spoke
In latter years of you: I did not fear
So soon to come again and you not here,
Our small town altered by a surly stroke
Of death, and the good book of many a year
Suddenly closed. New times, new wisdoms, new
Characters come, I know, but mourn for you.

In this the home of husbandry when first
I viewed all skill with young admiring zeal,
The pride of man and beast, of plough and wheel,
The soil, the seed, the yield so kindly nursed,
All that the country's casket could reveal
Of living treasure, foremost did you stand,
Great husbandman, master of widespread land.

Say it came natural—so yourself might say,
And nature's self could hardly have a sense
More sure and constant than has now gone hence
With you, for all that happens night and day,
And shine and shower, and tiny and immense,
In the ancient world of sap and grain and gourd,
Of dog and hog, of worm and bee and bird.

But not alone from these your oneness shines;
You had your pride, but it was on your lip
Most when remembering feats of sportsmanship,
Grand cricket, utmost prey of rods and lines,
Something of bowls, and then of spur and whip,
And autumn guns,—but cricket maybe most,
—Still in the slips I see you take your post.

Why, the small boy's first evening in the nets,
With bat almost above his ears, you came
To start him rightly in your classic game,
And lobbed the slow spun ball that always gets
The hopeful one—and first he tasted fame;
In Paradise I think you bowl so still,
Your art is feared by teams beyond the hill.

We follow, Father; and, as you approve,
We hasten slowly, as we are allowed.
Your old friends, daily grayer and more bowed,
Mildly along the lonelier pathway move,
And gathering, few now, chase the general cloud
By borrowing light you bore when you talked there
From the pink bud till orchard boughs are bare.

ALMSWOMEN

At Quincey's moat the squandering village ends,
And there in the almshouse dwell the dearest friends
Of all the village, two old dames that cling
As close as any trueloves in the spring.
Long, long ago they passed three-score-and-ten,
And in this doll's-house lived together then;
All things they have in common being so poor,
And their one fear, Death's shadow at the door.
Each sundown makes them mournful, each sunrise
Brings back the brightness in their failing eyes.

How happy go the rich fair-weather days
When on the roadside folk stare in amaze
At such a honeycomb of fruit and flowers
As mellows round their threshold; what long hours
They gloat upon their steepling hollyhocks,
Bee's balsams, feathery southernwood and stocks,
Fiery dragon's-mouths, great mallow leaves
For salves, and lemon-plants in bushy sheaves,
Shagged Esau's-hands with five green finger-tips.
Such old sweet names are ever on their lips.

As pleased as little children where these grow
In cobbled pattens and worn gowns they go,
Proud of their wisdom when on gooseberry shoots
They stuck egg shells to fright from coming fruits

The brisk-billed rascals; scanning still to see
Their neighbour owls saunter from tree to tree,
Or in the hushing half-light mouse the lane
Long-winged and lordly.

                  But when those hours wane
Indoors they ponder, scared by the harsh storm
Whose pelting saracens on the window swarm,
And listen for the mail to clatter past
And church clock's deep bay withering on the blast;
They feed the fire that flings its freakish light
On pictured kings and queens grotesquely bright,
Platters and pitchers, faded calendars
And graceful hourglass trim with lavenders.

Many a time they kiss and cry and pray
That both be summoned in the selfsame day,
And wiseman linnet tinkling in his cage
End too with them the friendship of old age,
And all together leave their treasured room
Some bell-like evening when the May's in bloom.

THE IDLERS

The gipsies lit their fires by the chalk-pit gate anew,
And the hoppled horses supped in the further dusk and dew;
The gnats flocked round the smoke like idlers as they were
And through the goss and bushes the owls began to churr.

An ell above the woods the last of sunset glowed
With a dusky gold that filled the pond beside the road;
The cricketers had done, the leas all silent lay,
And the carrier's clattering wheels went past and died
  away.

The gipsies lolled and gossiped, and ate their stolen swedes,
Made merry with mouth-organs, worked toys with piths of
  reeds:
The old wives puffed their pipes, nigh as black as their
  hair,
And not one of them all seemed to know the name of care.

THE WAGGONER

The old waggon drudges through the miry lane,
  By the skulking pond where the pollards frown,
Notched dumb surly images of pain;
  On a dulled earth the night droops down.

Wincing to slow and wistful airs
  The leaves on the shrubbed oaks know their hour,
And the unknown wandering spoiler bares
  The thorned black hedge of a mournful shower.

Small bodies fluster in the dead brown wrack
  As the stumbling shaft-horse jingles past
And the waggoner flicks his whip a crack;
  The odd light flares on shadows vast

Over the lodges and oasts and byres
  Of the darkened farm; the moment hangs wan
As though nature flagged and all desires.
  But in the dim court the ghost is gone

From the hug-secret yew to the penthouse wall
  And stooping there seems to listen to
The waggoner leading the gray to stall,
  As centuries past itself would do.

MOLE CATCHER

With coat like any mole's, as soft and black,
And hazel bows bundled beneath his arm,
With long-helved spade and rush bag on his back,
The trapper plods alone about the farm:
And spies new mounds in the ripe pasture-land,
And where the lob-worms writhe up in alarm
And easy sinks the spade, he takes his stand
Knowing the moles' dark highroad runs below:
Then sharp and square he chops the turf, and day
Gloats on the opened turnpike through the clay.

Out from his wallet hurry pin and prong,
And trap, and noose to tie it to the brow;
And then his grand arcanum, oily and strong,
Found out by his forefather years ago
To scent the peg and witch the moles along.
The bow is earthed and arched ready to shoot
And snatch the death-knot fast round the first mole
Who comes and snuffs well pleased and tries to root
Past the sly nose peg; back again is put
The mould, and death left smirking in the hole.
The old man goes and tallies all his snares
And finds the prisoners there and takes his toll.

And moles to him are only moles; but hares
See him afield and scarcely cease to nip
Their dinners, for he harms not them; he spares
The drowning fly that of his ale would sip
And throws the ant the crumbs of comradeship.
And every time he comes into his yard
Grey linnet knows he brings the groundsel sheaf,
And clatters round the cage to be unbarred,
And on his finger whistles twice as hard.—
What his old vicar says, is his belief,
In the side pew he sits and hears the truth;
And never misses once to ring his bell
On Sundays night and morn, nor once since youth
Has heard the chimes afield, but has heard tell
There's not a peal in England sounds so well.

THE POOR MAN'S PIG

Already fallen plum-bloom stars the green,
  And apple-boughs as knarred as old toads' backs
Wear their small roses ere a rose is seen;
  The building thrush watches old Job who stacks

The fresh-peeled osiers on the sunny fence,
  The pent sow grunts to hear him stumping by,
And tries to push the bolt and scamper thence,
  But her ringed snout still keeps her to the sty.

Then out he lets her run; away she snorts
  In bundling gallop for the cottage door,
With hungry hubbub begging crusts and orts,
  Then like the whirlwind bumping round once more;
Nuzzling the dog, making the pullets run,
And sulky as a child when her play's done.

THE PIKE

From shadows of rich oaks outpeer
The moss-green bastions of the weir,
Where the quick dipper forages
In elver-peopled crevices.
And a small runlet trickling down the sluice
Gossamer music tires not to unloose.

Else round the broad pool's hush
Nothing stirs.
Unless sometime a straggling heifer crush
Through the thronged spinney whence the pheasant whirs;
Or martins in a flash
Come with wild mirth to dip their magical wings,
While in the shallow some doomed bulrush swings
At whose hid root the diver vole's teeth gnash.
And nigh this toppling reed, still as the dead
The great pike lies, the murderous patriarch,
Watching the waterpit shelving and dark
Where through the plash his lithe bright vassals thread.

The rose-finned roach and bluish bream
And staring ruffe steal up the stream
Hard by their glutted tyrant, now
Still as a sunken bough.

He on the sandbank lies,
Sunning himself long hours
With stony gorgon eyes:
Westward the hot sun lowers.

Sudden the gray pike changes, and quivering poises for
    slaughter;
  Intense terror wakens around him, the shoals scud awry,
    but there chances
  A chub unsuspecting; the prowling fins quicken, in fury
    he lances;
And the miller that opens the hatch stands amazed at the
    whirl in the water.

CLOUDY JUNE

Above the hedge the spearman thistle towers
And thinks himself the god of all he sees;
But nettles jostle fearless where he glowers,
Like old and stained and sullen tapestries;
And elbowing hemlocks almost turn to trees,
Proud as the sweetbriar with her bubble flowers,
    Where puft green spider cowers
    To trap the toiling bees.

Here joy shall muse what melancholy tells,
And melancholy smile because of joy,
Whether the poppy breathe arabian spells
To make them friends, or whistling gipsy-boy
Sound them a truce that nothing comes to cloy.
No sunray burns through this slow cloud, nor swells
    Noise save the browsing-bells,
    Half sorrow and half joy.

Night comes; from fens where blind grey castles frown
A veiled moon ventures on the cavernous sky.
No stir, no tassel-tremble on the down:
Mood dims to nothing: atom-like I lie
Where nightjars burr and barking fox steps by
And hedgehogs talk and play in glimmering brown;
    Passions in such night drown,
    Nor tell me I am I.

THE MAY DAY GARLAND

Though folks no more go Maying
    Upon the dancing-green
With ale and cakes and music loud
    To crown the fairest queen,
Yet little ones to each gate go
    Before the clock tells noon,
And there the prettiest garlands show
    That Love can smile upon.

Their garlands are of paigles
    That flaunt their yellow heads
By dykesides where the pigeon broods
    And the nuzzling hedgehog beds—
Their ladysmocks shall nod in the sun
    And kingcups scent like mead,
And blue-bells' misty flame be spun
    With daisies' glittering brede.

And one will make her garland
    A crown for such a day,
One a harp, and one a heart
    (Lest hers be stolen away);
Cart-wheels never meant to turn
    And chip-hats never worn
And petal-tambourines shall earn
    A largess this May morn.

And for these courteous children,
  And Love that's ever a child,
The May should never fade tonight
  Could Time but be beguiled,
Could Time but see the beauty of
  These singing honied hours,
And lie in the sun adream while we
  Hid up his scythe in flowers!

BLUE BUTTERFLY

Here Lucy paused for the blue butterfly—
Blue with the mingled colours of the sky:
Here Lucy paused, and murmured to behold
His fingers long or feelers ringed with gold,
Ebony-ringed like cowboy's switches are,
And touched with sunset and its seraph star.

Frilled round he was, she bade me look, with white;
Over his body blossomed a soft light;
And in his wings a ruddiness remained
Like thunder skies, yet thence his sweet blue gained;
And when he shut his timid wings, then even
His undersides proclaimed a child of heaven,
Flecked with dark eyes, in paly circlets crowned.

Vetches of scarlet vein were legion round;
The speckled orchid grew, wild bean beside;
The aspens like a pebbled water sighed;
When he rose up to feathery fanning flight
And over sweetbriar dancing went from sight.
And here I see him yet, and Lucy's eye
Smiles on him from that day so past fled by,
And her delight so trembling and so true
Is whispering in my lonely walk anew.

HAWTHORN

Beneath that hawthorn shade the grass will hardly grow,
So many babes have played and kept the bare clay so,
So many loves delayed in the moonlight's ebb and flow—
    Daisy-chains and May beginnings,
    Fail not till I pass below.

The roots of this same thorn are polished like a stool,
Each grey and goblin horn craftwise beautiful,
And sometimes to adorn is left a tuft of wool—
    I envy still the merry runnings
    Of those that pass that way from school.

The moonlight through the may and the whisper fluttering
  there,
Like angels on their way to the lamp of pain and prayer,
Gleams and ripplings play, and we lay our forehead bare,
    For here the coolest, cleverest cunnings
    Know the unknown's wingèd air.

Come, little tiny child, here's white violets for thee,
Come, smiling beauty wild, love's the dryad of this tree,
And thou baptizèd mild, this thorny chapel see,
    And may I for all my sinnings
    Sit in this same sanctuary.

WHAT IS WINTER?

The haze upon the meadow
  Denies the dying year,
For the sun's within it, something bridal
  Is more than dreaming here.
There is no end, no severance,
No moment of deliverance,
    No quietus made,
Though quiet abounds and deliverance moves
    In that sunny shade.

What is winter? A word,
    A figure, a clever guess.
That time-word does not answer to
  This drowsy wakefulness.
The secret stream scorns interval
Though the calendar shouts one from the wall;
  The spirit has no last days;
And death is no more dead than this
  Flower-haunted haze.

THE SOUTH-WEST WIND

We stood by the idle weir,
  Like bells the waters played,
In the moonlight sleeping through the shire,
  As it would never fade:
So slept our shining peace of mind
Till rose a south-west wind.

How sorrow comes who knows?
  And here joy surely had been:
But joy like any wild wind blows
  From mountains none has seen,
And still its cloudy veilings throws
On the bright road it goes.

The black-plumed poplars swung
  Softly across the sky;
The ivy sighed, the river sung,
  Woolpacks were wafting high.
The moon her golden tinges flung
On these she straight was lost among.

O south-west wind of the soul,
  That brought such new delight,
And passing by in music stole
  Love's rich and trusting light,
Would that we thrilled to thy least breath,
Now all is still as death.

A PROSPECT OF SWANS

Walking the river way to change our note
From the hard season and from harder care,
      Marvelling we found the swans,
The swans on sullen swollen dykes afloat
Or moored on tussocks, a full company there,
White breasts and necks, advance and poise and stir
Filling the scene, while rays of steel and bronze
From the far dying sun touched the dead reeds.

So easy was the manner of each one,
So sure and wise the course of all their needs,
So free their unity, in that level sun
And floodland tipped with sedge and osiery,
It might have been where man was yet to be,
Some mere where none but swans were ever kings,
Where gulls might hunt, a wide flight in from sea,
And page-like small birds come: all innocent wings.

O picture of some first divine intent,
O young world which perhaps was modelled thus,
      Where even hard winter meant
No disproportion, hopeless hungers none,
And set no task which could not well be done.
Now this primeval pattern gleamed at us
Right near the town's black smoke-towers and the roar
Of trains bearing the sons of man to war.

NATURE'S ADORNINGS

Whence is such glory? who would know
The slough and swamp could yield it? Forth it leaps
Above the wreck of woods, where no path is,
Illuminate, yellow flag in flower, true prince
Of desolate places. If a child pass here,
Whose dreams have grown unhappy with the ghost
Of this feared swamp, immediately the flame
Of courage in green stem and golden wreath
Shall break that spell.
                            The splendours of the world
Are such that number and inquiry fade;
There is no reason for them but themselves,
That they are such, is felt as wonderful
Compared with what they grow from; so it is.

The child soul-struck with the yellow flag's new fire
In the next moment sees his kingfisher,
Than stained glass brighter, all his bravery on,
Of all our small birds only so adorned,
A tense blue instant; and this sumptuousness—
To haunt a tiny trampled pasture brook.

In that same brook, though, several splendours live;
The perch, a champion armed and blazing, scorning
The common shoal, empurples the gray sands.
What flawless lustrous life the swan's breast sheds
In subtler shinings on the gazing child;
And then, mocking the other panoplies,
The dragon-fly zooms round, a diamond nerve.

On him and them the summer's frown will fall,
And cloud their jewels with ereboean gloom,
Thunder's slow heavy nihilistic wave.
Thence, even thence, the glory springs in swift
Splendour of iris'd lightning; thus once more
The slough and swamp of nature yields this wild
Royal extravagance, this conquering pride
In singular blazonry, to witch the world.

COUNTRY SALE

Under the thin green sky, the twilight day,
The old home lies in public sad array,
Its time being come, the lots ranged out in rows,
And to each lot a ghost. The gathering grows
With every minute, neckcloths and gold pins;
Poverty's purples; red necks, horny skins,
Odd peeping eyes, thin lips and hooking chins.

Then for the skirmish, and the thrusting groups
Bidding for tubs and wire and chicken coops,
While yet the women hang apart and eye
Their friends and foes and reckon who will buy.
The noisy field scarce knows itself, not one
Takes notice of the old man's wavering moan
Who hobbles with his hand still brushing tears
And cries how this belonged here sixty years,
And picks his brother's picture from the mass
Of frames; and still from heap to heap folks pass.

The strife of tongues even tries the auctioneer,
Who, next the dealer smirking to his leer,
A jumped-up jerky cockerel on his box,
Runs all his rigs, cracks all his jokes and mocks;
'Madam, now never weary of well-doing,'
The heavy faces gleam to hear him crowing.
And swift the old home's fading. Here he bawls
The white four-poster, with its proud recalls,
But we on such old-fashioned lumber frown;
'Passing away at a florin,' grins the clown.

Here Baskett's Prayer Book with his black and red
Finds no more smile of welcome than the bed,
Though policeman turn the page with wisdom's looks:
The hen-wives see no sense in such old books.
Here painted trees and well-feigned towers arise
And ships before the wind, that sixpence buys.

All's sold; then hasty vanmen pile and rope
Their loads, and ponies stumble up the slope
And all are gone, the trampled paddock's bare;
The children round the buildings run and blare,
Thinking what times these are! not knowing how
The heavy-handed fate has brought them low,
Till quartern loaf be gone too soon today,
And none is due tomorrow. Long, then, play,
And make the lofts re-echo through the eve,
And sweeten so the bitter taking-leave.

So runs the world away. Years hence shall find
The mother weeping to her lonely mind,
In some new place, thin set with makeshift gear,
For the home she had before the fatal year;
And still to this same anguish she'll recur,
Reckoning up her fine old furniture,
The tall clock with his church-bell time of day,
The mirror where so deep the image lay,
The china with its rivets numbered all,
Seeming to have them in her hands—poor soul,
Trembling and crying how these, loved so long,
So beautiful, all went for an old song.

NO CONTINUING CITY

The train with its smoke and its rattle went on,
And the heavy-cheeked porter wheeled off his mixed load;
She shivered, and stood as if loth to be gone,
Staring this way and that—on the watery road,
And the inn with its arbour all naked and bleak,
And the weir churning foam, and the meaningless oast;
Till her husband turned back, and he stroked her pale
   cheek.
'O dear,' murmured she, 'must we go? but at most

        I shall never live here
        Above half a year.'

And he with eyes keen as his bright singing mind,
While the cab tumbled on through the drifts of brown
   mist,
Shared her trouble; but knew that his future designed
A loftier life, could they meantime exist:
Then he sparkled and rested, and kissed his young sweet,
And they turned to the village, and stopped at the green
To enter the schoolhouse with echoing feet;
And she scanned, and she planned, though she murmured
   between
        'I can never stay here
        Above half a year.'

And now forty years of his scholars have passed,
Dunce, sluggard and prizeman; the master remains:
He has built a new wing; and the school cap's recast;

43

And he makes his old jokes about beauty and brains.
And *she* speaks of home, but it is not this place,
But where a white waterfall springs down the crags,
And she goes to the garret, and stares into space,
Yet smiles when he finds her. The village tongue wags,

'She'll never be here
At this time next year.'

44

THE CHILD'S GRAVE

I came to the churchyard where pretty Joy lies
  On a morning in April, a rare sunny day;
Such bloom rose around, and so many birds' cries,
  That I sang for delight as I followed the way.

I sang for delight in the ripening of spring,
  For dandelions even were suns come to earth;
Not a moment went by but a new lark took wing
  To wait on the season with melody's mirth.

Love-making birds were my mates all the road,
  And who would wish surer delight for the eye
Than to see pairing goldfinches gleaming abroad
  Or yellowhammers sunning on paling and sty?

And stocks in the almswomen's garden were blown
  With rich Easter roses each side of the door;
The lazy white owls in the glade cool and lone
  Paid calls on their cousins in the elm's chambered core.

This peace, then, and happiness thronged me around.
  Nor could I go burdened with grief, but made merry
Till I came to the gate of that overgrown ground
  Where scarce once a year sees the priest come to bury.

Over the mounds stood the nettles in pride,
  And, where no fine flowers, there kind weeds dared to
    wave,
It seemed but as yesterday she lay by my side,
  And now my dog ate of the grass on her grave.

He licked my hand wondering to see me muse so,
  And wished I would lead on the journey or home,
As though not a moment of spring were to go
  In brooding; but I stood, if her spirit might come

And tell me her life, since we left her that day
  In the white lilied coffin, and rained down our tears;
But the grave held no answer, though long I should stay;
  How strange that this clay should mingle with hers!

So I called my good dog, and went on my way;
  Joy's spirit shone then in each flower I went by,
And clear as the noon, in coppice and ley,
  Her sweet dawning smile and her violet eye!

46

FOR THE COUNTRY LIFE

No sunbeam clearer
　　Than through our garret window ever leapt;
The pearmain blossomed
　　Waiting for us who lightly slept
　　And often in our stockings crept

Into the scent of the morning,
　　The mist before the boundless day;
Just for the fun we filled a bucket
　　In that white well whose springs allay
　　　　Us on our way

To join great hearts through thicker mist of
　　　　battle,
　　Chaos of wills; the smoke will yield.
The thing is only
　　For us to bring to the wise ones in the field
　　The strength so early revealed:

And with those sunbeams,
　　Those swallows under the eaves, and din
Of cockerels and larks and cuckoos
　　Let the battle for men begin,
　　And I think we shall win.

WAR REMEMBERED

Morning, if this late withered light can claim
Some kindred with that merry flame
Which the young day was wont to fling through
   space!
Agony stares from each gray face.
And yet the day is come; stand down! stand down!
Your hands unclasp from rifles while you can,
The frost has pierced them to the bended bone?
Why, see old Stevens there, that iron man,
Melting the ice to shave his grotesque chin:
Go ask him, shall we win?
I never liked this bay, some foolish fear
Caught me the first time that I came in here;
That dugout fallen in awakes, perhaps,
Some formless haunting of some corpse's chaps.
True, and wherever we have held the line,
There were such corners, seeming-saturnine
    For no good cause.
               Now where Haymarket starts,
That is no place for soldiers with weak hearts;
The minenwerfers have it to the inch.
Look, how the snowdust whisks along the road,
Piteous and silly; the stones themselves must flinch
In this east wind; the low sky like a load
Hangs over—a dead-weight. But what a pain
Must gnaw where its clay cheek
Crushes the shell-chopped trees that fang the plain—
The ice-bound throat gulps out a gargoyle shriek.
The wretched wire before the village line
Rattles like rusty brambles or dead bine,

And then the daylight oozes into dun;
Black pillars, those are trees where roadways run.
Even Ypres now would warm our souls; fond fool,
Our tour's but one night old, seven more to cool!
O screaming dumbness, O dull clashing death,
Shreds of dead grass and willows, homes and men,
Watch as you will, men clench their chattering teeth
And freeze you back with that one hope, disdain.

AT SENLIS ONCE

O how comely it was and how reviving,
When with clay and with death no longer striving
   Down firm roads we came to houses
   With women chattering and green grass thriving.

Now though rains in a cataract descended,
We could glow, with our tribulation ended—
   Count not days, the present only
   Was thought of, how could it ever be expended?

Clad so cleanly, this remnant of poor wretches
Picked up life like the hens in orchard ditches,
   Gazed on the mill-sails, heard the church-bell,
   Found an honest glass all manner of riches.

How they crowded the barn with lusty laughter,
Hailed the pierrots and shook each shadowy rafter,
   Even could ridicule their own sufferings,
   Sang as though nothing but joy came after!

AN INFANTRYMAN

Painfully writhed the few last weeds upon those houseless
   uplands,
      Cleft pods had dropt their blackened seeds into the
      trampled clay,
Wind and rain were running loose, and icy flew the whip-
   lash;
      Masked guns like autumn thunder drummed the out-
      cast year away.

Hidden a hundred yards ahead with winter's blinding
   passion,
      The mule-beat track appeared half dead, even war's
      hot blood congealed;

The half-dug trenches brimmed like troughs, the camps lay
   slushed and empty,
      Unless those bitter whistlings proved Death's army in
      the field.

Over the captured ridge above the hurt battalion waited,
      And hardly had sense left to prove if ghost or living
      passed
From hole to hole with sunken eyes and slow ironic orders,
      While fiery fountains burst and clanged—and there
      your lot was cast.

Yet I saw your health and youth go brightening to the
   vortex,
      The ghosts on guard, the storm uncouth were then no
      match for you;
You smiled, you sang, your courage rang, and to this day
   I hear it,
      Sunny as a May-day dance, along that spectral
      avenue.

THE LATE STAND-TO

I thought of cottages nigh brooks
    Whose aspens loved to shine and swirl,
Of chubby babies' wondering looks
    Above the doorboards, and the girl
Who blossomed like the morning sky,
    With clear light like a lily made;
She dipt her bucket and went by,
    Where bright the unwithering water played.

No water ever ran so blithe
    As that same mill-tail stream, I'd say,
And life as laughing danced as lithe
    And twinkled on as many a day.
The wonder seemed that summer waned,
    So full it filled the giant sphere,
But skulls chill on where warm blood reigned
    And even such summers must grow sere.

I heard the bell brag on the west
    And whisper on the eastern wind,
And hated how it found the nest
    That Time was never meant to find:
Though many an afternoon blue-hung
    Like sultry smoke with drowsy heat
There came the bell-cote's scheming tongue
    Till gipsy-boys that slouched down street

With roach on withy rods impaled
   Had flown, and swallows met to fly,
And yellow light and leaves prevailed
   And trouble roved the evening sky.
But spite of ghosts who shook their hair
   In clouds and stalked through darker plains,
Still to the wood bridge I'd repair
   Ere autumn palsied into rains.

The fish turned over in the shoal,
   A flash of summer! then came she,
Who when green leaves were lapping cool
   So like a lily dazzled me;
Her basketful of mushrooms got,
   She passed, she called me by my name,
And now whole myriads are forgot
   But kindly Nell will seem the same

Down to my death! Long tarry, Sun,
   That shone upon us two that day,
And autumn's honey breath live on
   The last sighed air that leaves me clay!—
Clay! clay! the packing bullets mocked
   And split the breastwork by my head,
And into aching senses shocked
   I gave Stand-To! the east was red.

THE ANCRE AT HAMEL: AFTERWARDS

Where tongues were loud and hearts were
    light
  I heard the Ancre flow;
Waking oft at the mid of night
  I heard the Ancre flow.
I heard it crying, that sad rill,
  Below the painful ridge,
By the burnt unraftered mill
  And the relic of a bridge.

And could this sighing water seem
  To call me far away,
And its pale word dismiss as dream
  The voices of today?
The voices in the bright room chilled
  And that mourned on alone;
The silence of the full moon filled
  With that brook's troubling tone.

The struggling Ancre had no part
  In these new hours of mine,
And yet its stream ran through my heart;
  I heard it grieve and pine,
As if its rainy tortured blood
  Had swirled into my own,
When by its battered bank I stood
  And shared its wounded moan.

THEIR VERY MEMORY

Hear, O hear,
They were as the welling waters,
  Sound, swift, clear,
They were all the running waters'
  Music down the greenest valley.

Might words tell
What an echo sung within me?
  What proud bell
Clangs a note of what within me
  Pealed to be with those enlisted?

When they smiled,
Earth's inferno changed and melted
  Greenwood mild;
Every village where they halted
  Shone with them through square and alley.

Now my mind
Faint and few records their showings,
  Brave, strong, kind—
I'd unlock you all their doings
  But the keys are lost and twisted.

This still grows,
Through my land or dull or dazzling
  Their spring flows;
But to think of them's a fountain,
  Tears of joy and music's rally.

1916 SEEN FROM 1921

Tired with dull grief, grown old before my day,
I sit in solitude and only hear
Long silent laughters, murmurings of dismay,
The lost intensities of hope and fear;
In those old marshes yet the rifles lie,
On the thin breastwork flutter the grey rags,
The very books I read are there—and I
Dead as the men I loved, wait while life drags

Its wounded length from those sad streets of war
Into green places here, that were my own;
But now what once was mine is mine no more,
I seek such neighbours here and I find none.
With such strong gentleness and tireless will
Those ruined houses seared themselves in me,
Passionate I look for their dumb story still,
And the charred stub outspeaks the living tree.

I rise up at the singing of a bird
And scarcely knowing slink along the lane,
I dare not give a soul a look or word
Where all have homes and none's at home in vain:
Deep red the rose burned in the grim redoubt,
The self-sown wheat around was like a flood,
In the hot path the lizard lolled time out,
The saints in broken shrines were bright as blood.

Sweet Mary's shrine between the sycamores!
There we would go, my friend of friends and I,
And snatch long moments from the grudging wars,
Whose dark made light intense to see them by.
Shrewd bit the morning fog, the whining shots
Spun from the wrangling wire; then in warm swoon
The sun hushed all but the cool orchard plots,
We crept in the tall grass and slept till noon.

ILLUSIONS

Trenches in the moonlight, in the lulling moonlight
Have had their loveliness; when dancing dewy grasses
Caressed us passing along their earthly lanes;
When the crucifix hanging over was strangely illumined,
And one imagined music, one even heard the brave bird
In the sighing orchards flute above the weedy well.
There are such moments; forgive me that I note them,
Nor gloze that there comes soon the nemesis of beauty,
In the fluttering relics that at first glimmer wakened
Terror—no-man's ditch suddenly forking:
There, the enemy's best with bombs and brains and
    courage!
—Softly, swiftly, at once be animal and angel—
But O no, no, they're Death's malkins dangling in the
    wire
    For the moon's interpretation.

THE BRANCH LINE

Professing loud energy, out of the junction departed
The branch-line engine. The small train rounded the bend
Watched by us pilgrims of summer, and most by me, —
Who had known this picture since first my travelling
    started,
And knew it as sadly pleasant, the usual end
Of singing returns to beloved simplicity.

The small train went from view behind the plantation,
Monotonous,— but there's a grace in monotony!
I felt its journey, I watched in imagination
Its brown smoke spun with sunshine wandering free
Past the great weir with its round flood-mirror beneath,
And where the magpie rises from orchard shadows,
And among the oasts, and like a rosy wreath
Mimicking children's flower-play in the meadows.

The thing so easy, so daily, of so small stature
Gave me another picture: of war's warped face
Where still the sun and the leaf and the lark praised
    Nature,
But no little engine bustled from place to place;
When summer succeeded summer, yet only ghosts
Or tomorrow's ghosts could venture hand or foot
In the track between the terrible telegraph-posts, —
The end of all things lying between the hut
Which lurked this side, and the shattered local train
That.
    So easy it was; and should that come again— .

FAR EAST

FAR EAST

Old hamlets with your fragrant flowers
    And honey for the bee,
Your curtained taverns, chiming towers,
Droning songs and twilight hours
    And nodding industry—

Fine fields, wide-lapped, whose loveliest-born
    Day's first bright cohort finds,
And steals away; whose lustier corn
The red-faced churl invades at morn
    And proud as Caesar binds—

Uplands and groves that from the West
    Have the last word for me,
Think not your image in my breast
Was darkened when I sang my best
    Beside an Eastern sea.

Beside an Eastern sea the pines
    In tufty spinneys drowse,
The firefly-grass beneath them shines
Blue-lanterned, and the chaliced vines
    Climb witch-like to the boughs;

And girdled green there bask the plains
    Where, with his timeless smiles,
And mushroom-hat, brown Vigour gains
His splindling roots, his haulms, his grains—
    The Oriental Giles.

He serves a god much like your own,
  Who, peeping from the rows,
Brings gourds the greatest ever grown,
And peerless pumpkins; smooths the down
  Of these fruits, lacquers those.

Thence the young child at home awaits,
  Bright-peering as a mouse,
Her share of country delicates,
And chatters bold to her young mates
  About the smoky house.

The bronze cicada twangs all day,
  And the silver-soft at night
Cools the snake's thicket by the way
Where heaps the sturdy disarray
  Of husbandry's delight.

In rural music bold or frail
  Contentment's anthem fills,
And, roving the rude-ripened vale,
If restless spirits sometime fail,
  Here too are heavenly hills.

Sleep's master-dream there stands alone:
  The mount of East and West!
The still hour come, his monstrous cone
Is a timid flower this morning blown,
  Now folded like the rest.

ELEGY

The Chinese tombs,
Some, squares of shrubby trees, some, peaks and mounds,
But more like tile-roofed huts and cottages,
Rise here and there among the fertile grounds.
The spring day blooms
Palely above them, and a warm tear falls
At moments from her opening eyes upon
Those hillocks and those walls;
The encircling wheat and beans as yet are wan,
With the dim stress of winter hardly gone;
The green corn waves
With the thin wind in its tall shroudage flowing,
Above those graves; the living labourer's hoeing
Ends at those graves.

PETALS

An unseen hand
    Is playing with the blossoms there:
    We hear or heard across from there
A singing from a far-off land.

    What child of chance
Is fashioning that flower-fountain white,
Is scattering snowy mountain-light
    Where these familiar branches dance?

    So play, so sing,
Among our city shapes of time,
While thought by thought escapes from time
    Invisible you, love-thief of spring.

A JAPANESE EVENING

Round us the pines are darkness
That with a wild melodious piping rings
While in the ditches
Slow as toads in English gardens
The little landcrabs move.
We re-discover our path,
And, coming to the cottage, are greeted
With hierophantic usherings and oracles,
And a grin behind the screen, I imagine.
We guess full fathom five, and take up the
    chopsticks.
The metal-blue cucumber slices,
Rice, string beans,
And green tea over,
The housekeeper looking kindly amazement
At the master of the house
Soon makes all shipshape.
After all, they possess an American clock,
A very fine, a high-collar clock.
She sits on the mat, awaiting the next oddity.

Lanterns moon the outer darkness,
And merrily in come floating
(So gently they foot the honourable straw)
Three young girls, who sit them down.
A conference;
Almost the Versailles of the Far East:
The master, beaming,
His white hair in the lamplight seeming brighter
    with his pleasure,

Asks me what I call *O tsuki sama*.
Moon.
Mooon.
Moon.
He has got it; right first time,
But not the next.
Moooni.
(The housekeeper cannot suppress her giggles,
Okashii, she says, and so it`is.)
We now pass naturally to the
Electric Light.
But he will not have that,
There are no things like that in heaven and earth
In his philology.
I repeat—what I said,
He repeats—what he said.
We close at Erecturiku Rightu.
We fasten also on:
The cat, who becomes catsu,
The dog, who proceeds doggi,
(And I suspect has rabies beginning);
Himself, O-Ji-San, Orudu Genturuman,
And all sorts of enigmas.

The girls are quicker, more nimble-throated,
And will reproduce exactly the word, but he lays
    the law down;
Having re-orientated Fan,
Which they pronounced Fan,
Into Weino,
He instructs them how it ought to be pronounced,
Obediently young Japan reiterates his decision,

Not without an ocular hint to the stranger
That they have concealed the other rendering in
   their minds . . .
I hear their voices tinkling, lessening
Over the firefly grass,
Along the seething sand below the pines,
At the end of the entertainment.

A HONG KONG HOUSE

'And now a dove and now a dragon-fly
Came to the garden; sometimes as we sat
Outdoors in twilight noiseless owl and bat
Flew shadowily by.
It was no garden,— so adust, red-dry
The rock-drift soil was, no kind root or sweet
Scent-subtle flower would house there, but I own
At certain seasons, burning bright,
Full-blown,
Some trumpet-purple blooms blazed at the sun's
     huge light.'

And then? tell more.
'The handy lizard and quite nimble toad
Had courage often to explore
Our large abode.
The infant lizard whipped across the wall
To his own objects; how to slide like him
Along the upright plane and never fall,
Ascribe to Eastern whim.
The winged ants flocked to our lamp, and shed
Their petally wings, and walked and crept instead.

'The palm-tree-top soared into the golden blue
And soaring skyward drew
Its straight stem etched with many rings,
And one broad holm-like tree whose name I never
     knew

Was decked through all its branches with broidering
    leaves
Of pattern-loving creepers; fine warblings
And gong-notes thence were sounded at our eaves
By clever birds one very seldom spied,
Except when they, of one tree tired,
Into another new-desired,
Over the lawn and playthings chose to glide.'

TO THE NEW JAPAN

'Come, little babe, come, silly soul'—
The old song speaks my heart for me
Wherever I see them as I stroll,
These buds of rosy infancy,
Japan's young children, staring shy
Or not so shy, from mother's back
Or doorstep-side, as we go by,—
If love could bring them all they lack!

Come, serious youth, and burdened deep
With yesterday's left loads as well
As those which sent you late to sleep,
And roused you soon; could age dispel
Some part of those, could faith express
Strong exhortation to each one,
It might be, from the wilderness
Each with a gayer rhythm would run.

Come, life and thought, come, skill and charm,
Here in the land which far-born we,
In rushing street or brown-roofed farm,
Have eyes and minds and hearts to see,
And whence we learn calm light; come all,
And let us, as we can, declare:—
For young, for old, a spirit-call
Even now, bright music, stirs the air.

CHINESE PAPER-KNIFE

For the first time ever, and only now
  (Long waiting where I should see)
The tiny carved bird, the bony bough
  Start sharp into life for me.

Why not until now, why suddenly now
  This recognition? Replies
The bird must know who from that bough
  Holds me with staring eyes:

The owl once more, but this time found
  In foliage strange to me.
Fantastic branches warp around
  From the scaly uptwisting tree.

A trifle, ah yes: but the carver achieved
  A forest dream where flies
In and out the boughs so various-leaved
  This bird with pinhead eyes.

Then praisèd be this today whose light
  Revealed this fabulous tree
And original owl, which many a night
  Will lead into mystery.

POETRY AND POETS

THE ENGLISH POETS

I looked across the fields and saw a light
　Abroad through all the morning earth and air,
A hue of heaven!—I thought it common sight;
　Was radiant thence and dreamed all people were.

A hue of heaven! or passion of old earth,
　Triumphant in the pastoral long played there,
Memory of wakes and wooings and May mirth
　When Lear was young; so shone my earth and air.

Yet to no words I set my revery;
　Loved well the landscape, but as though its prime
For all eyes bloomed from cloud and shepherd's tree,
　For me would bloom, as trees would, all my time—

Till years had changed my gazing. Then as one
  Wakes from a dream and sighing would renew
The happy dream, but then! it is clean gone,
  I knew my loss, I sighed for the darling hue.

How many doting eyes of poets dead
  Have known and lost the Spirit of this sweet land
Who to young wonder glows! and as I read,
  Longing in past enchanted vales to stand,

From pages hid away by time, or crowned
  With timeless laurels, oft on a sudden arose
The mist of magic, and old haunted ground
  Shone with the Spirit who to young wonder glows.

Soon come, soon gone! and yet the brief disclose
  Sweetened my days, and in desire I grew
The constant suppliant and the friend of those
  From whose love's annals, known to all or few,

By virtue of that true and earnest love,
  The wandering light might kindle here and there;
In halt harsh phrase or Muses' treasure-trove,
  In warmest ecstasy or recountings bare.

And shall I ever pass the humblest name
  Of honest English song for England sung,
When from the uncouth shrine to me might flame
  The spirit fire that keeps our England young?

CLARE'S GHOST

Pitch-dark night shuts in, and the rising gale
    Is full of the presage of rain,
    And there comes a withered wail
    From the wainscot and jarring pane,
    And a long funeral surge
    Like a wood-god's dirge,
Like the wash of the shoreward tides, from the firs on the
       crest.

The shaking hedges blacken, the last gold flag
    Lowers from the West;
The Advent bell moans wild like a witch hag
    In the storm's unrest,
And the lychgate lantern's candle weaves a shroud,
    And the unlatched gate shrieks loud.

Up fly the smithy sparks, but are baffled from soaring
    By the pelting scurry, and ever
As puff the bellows, a multitude more outpouring
    Die foiled in the endeavour.

And a stranger stands with me here in the glow
Chinked through the door, and marks
    The sparks
Perish in whirlpool wind, and if I go
To the delta of cypress, where the glebe gate cries,
I see him there, with his streaming hair
    And his eyes
Piercing beyond our human firmament,
Lit with a burning deathless discontent.

HIGH ELMS, BRACKNELL

Two buds we took from thousands more
   In Shelley's garden overgrown,
   Beneath our roof they are now full-blown,
A royal pair, a scarlet twain
   Through whose warm lives our thoughts explore
   Back through long years to come at one
Which Shelley loved in sun or rain.

Fleeting's the life of these strange flowers,
   Enchanting poppies satin-frilled,
   Dark-purple hearts, yet these rebuild
A distant world, a summer dead*
   Millions of poppy-lives ere ours,
   And Shelley's visionary towers
Come nearer in their Indian red;

Not but some shadow of despair
   In this dark purple ominous
   From that high summer beckons us;
And such a shadow, such a doom
   Was lurking in the garden there.
   We could not name the incubus,
Save that it haunted Shelley's home.

Was it that through the same glass door
   With weary heart, uncertain why,
   But first discerning love can die,
Harriet had moved alone and slow;
   Or Shelley in the moonlight bore
   The cold curt word Necessity
From poppies that had seemed to know?

Then tracing the lost path between
   The herbs and flowers and wilderness,
   Whose was the phantom of our guess
Drawn by that quiet deserted pond
   With little boat, now scarcely seen
   For tears or bodings? Whose distress
Darkened the watery diamond?

* In 1813.

THOUGHTS OF THOMAS HARDY

'Are you looking for someone, you who come pattering
Along this empty corridor, dead leaf, to my door,
And before I had noticed that leaves were now dying?'

> 'No, nobody; but the way was open.
> The wind blew that way.
> There was no other way.
> And why your question?'

'O, I felt I saw someone with forehead bent downward
At the sound of your coming,
And he in that sound
Looked aware of a vaster threne of decline,
And considering a law of all life.
Yet he lingered, one lovingly regarding
Your particular fate and experience, poor leaf.'

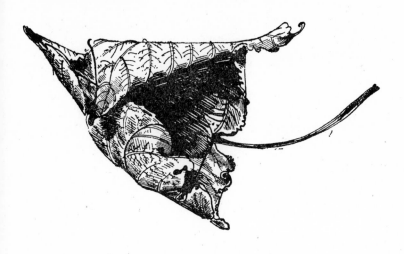

In the meadow by the mill
    I'd make my ballad,
Tunes to that would whistle shrill
And beat the blackbird's ringing bill.
But surely the innocent spring has died,
The sultry noon has hushed the bird,
The jingling word, the turn and glide
All in that meadow must have died.
For that, the fuller speech of song
    Has charmed me,
And lulled my lonely hours along;
Through beauty's truth that leads today
    My longing trials
Shone then like dewdrops in my way
When 'Nature painted all things gay.'

MYSTERIES

THE BROOK

Up, my jewel! let's away
   There where none but young love lingers;
Bells are ringing folks to pray,
   But ours are older bells and ringers,
Where the stream's broken gleams
   Glance through tresses of green willow,
Fishes glide, and beside
   Flowers laugh, blue, white and yellow.

On this bridge 'tis good to lean,
   Cooling care with the dance and dripple,
Nor do you your lovelight screen
   But outgleam the dimpling ripple:
Minim waves, nutshell caves,
   Cataracts over pebbles hurling,
To whose falls on the walls
   Myriad mimic suns go twirling!

But what dying dying fall,
   What low ebbing syllables
Hear I now? what ghosts recall
   Their shadowing piteous chronicles?
O my dear! This pale fear—
   Sun so cold, so dark! O never—
My life stream's broken gleams
   Stolen into the gulf for ever!

A BRIDGE

'Beyond the church there stands a bridge,'
  The greyhead said in his thin moan,
'And the river below's nor quick nor slow,
  And the green weed waves beside his stone.'

The summer's dust in curling gust
  Had floured me like a miller's man,

And on the hot bridge-wall I leant
   To watch how sweet the water ran.

Then all things crumbled, with a roar
   Mountains of waters champed and hurled;
The sluices crashed and deluge flashed
   And spun me through a gasping world

Of black and green heads breaking loose,
   With hideous bubbles, bolting eyes,
And rage and race, and white grimace,
   And sidelong monstrous agonies.

Then sick and scarlet wheeled the sun
   Above a slackened seething flood,
And in red creeks poked fish with beaks,
   And shell-strong claws scooped the swart mud,

And congregate in sharkish hate
   Hundreds of demon slayers basked
In the mid gulf, scaled thunder-bronze,
   And their swift brains one victim asked.

'Why, there you see the bridge again,'
   The grey ghost said. 'How time has flown!
The pools lie clear this time of year,
   And the green weed's lazy beside his stone.'

DEATH OF CHILDHOOD BELIEFS

There the puddled lonely lane,
    Lost among the red swamp sallows,
Gleams through drifts of summer rain
    Down to ford the sandy shallows,
Where the dewberry brambles crane.

And the stream in cloven clay
    Round the bridging sheep-gate stutters,
Wind-spun leaves burn silver-grey,
    Far and wide the blue moth flutters
Over swathes of warm new hay.

Scrambling boys with mad to-do
  Paddle in the sedges' hem,
Ever finding joy anew;
  Clocks toll time out—not for them,
With what years to frolic through!

How shall I return and how
  Look once more on those old places!
For Time's cloud is on me now
  That each day, each hour effaces
Visions once on every bough.

Stones could talk together then,
  Jewels lay for hoes to find,
Each oak hid King Charles agen,
  Ay, nations in his powdered rind;
Sorcery lived with homeless men.

Spider Dick, with cat's green eyes
  That could pierce stone walls, has flitted—
By some hedge he shakes and cries,
  A lost man, half-starved, half-witted,
Whom the very stoats despise.

Trees on hill-tops then were Palms,
  Closing pilgrims' arbours in;
David walked there singing Psalms,
  Out of the clouds white seraphin
Leaned to watch us fill our bin.

Where's the woodman now to tell
　　Will o'the Wisp's odd fiery anger?
Where's the ghost to toll the bell
　　Startling midnight with its clangour
Till the wind seemed but a knell?

Drummers jumping from the tombs
　　Banged and thumped all through the town,
Past shut shops and silent rooms
　　While the flaming spires fell down:—
Now but dreary thunder booms.

Smuggler trapped in headlong spate,
　　Smuggler's mare with choking whinney,
Well I knew your fame, your fate;
　　By the ford and shaking spinney
Where you perished I would wait.

Half in glory, half in fear,
　　While the fierce flood, trough and crest,
Whirled away the shepherd's gear,
　　And sunset wildfire coursed the west,
Crying Armageddon near.

THE TIME IS GONE

The time is gone when we could throw
  Our angle in the sleepy stream,
And nothing more desired to know
  Than was it roach or was it bream?
Sitting there in such a mute delight,
The kingfisher would come and on the rods
  alight.

Or, hurrying through the dewy hay
  Without a thought but to make haste,
We came to where the old ring lay
  And bats and balls seemed heaven at least.
With our laughing and our giant strokes
The echoes clacked among the chestnuts and
  the oaks.

When the spring came up we got
  And out among old Ammet Hills
Blossoms, aye and pleasures sought
  And found! bloom withers, pleasure chills;
Then geographers along wild brooks
We named the tumbling-bays and creeks and
  horse-shoe crooks.

But one day I found a man
  Leaning on the bridge's rail;
Dared his downward face to scan,
  And awestruck wondered what could ail
An elder, blest with all the gifts of years,
In such a happy place to shed such bitter tears.

TIMBER

In the avenues of yesterday
A tree might have a thing to say.
 Horsemen then heard
 From the branches a word
That sent them serious on their way.

A tree,— a beam, a box, a crutch,
Costing so little or so much;
 Wainscot or stair,
 Barge, baby's chair,
A pier, a flute, a mill, a hutch.

That tree uprooted lying there
Will make such things with knack and care,
 Unless you hear
 From its boughs too clear
The word that has whitened the traveller's hair.

THE MIDNIGHT SKATERS

The hop-poles stand in cones,
　The icy pond lurks under,
The pole-tops steeple to the thrones
　Of stars, sound gulfs of wonder;
But not the tallest there, 'tis said,
Could fathom to this pond's black bed.

Then is not death at watch
　Within those secret waters?
What wants he but to catch
　Earth's heedless sons and daughters?
With but a crystal parapet
Between, he has his engines set.

Then on, blood shouts, on, on,
　Twirl, wheel and whip above him,
Dance on this ball-floor thin and wan,
　Use him as though you love him;
Court him, elude him, reel and pass,
And let him hate you through the glass.

THE SUNLIT VALE

I saw the sunlit vale, and the pastoral fairy-tale;
The sweet and bitter scent of the may drifted by;
And never have I seen such a bright bewildering green,
   But it looked like a lie,
   Like a kindly meant lie.

When gods are in dispute, one a Sidney, one a brute,
It would seem that human sense might not know, might
    not spy;
But though nature smile and feign where foul play has
     stabbed and slain,
   There's a witness, an eye,
   Nor will charms blind that eye.

Nymph of the upland song and the sparkling leafage
    young,
For your merciful desire with these charms to beguile,
For ever be adored; muses yield you rich reward;
   But you fail, though you smile—
   That other does not smile.

REPORT ON EXPERIENCE

I have been young, and now am not too old;
And I have seen the righteous forsaken,
His health, his honour and his quality taken.
   This is not what we were formerly told.

I have seen a green country, useful to the race,
Knocked silly with guns and mines, its villages
  vanished,
Even the last rat and last kestrel banished—
   God bless us all, this was peculiar grace.

I knew Seraphina; Nature gave her hue,
Glance, sympathy, note, like one from Eden.
I saw her smile warp, heard her lyric deaden;
   She turned to harlotry;— this I took to be new.

Say what you will, our God sees how they run.
These disillusions are His curious proving
That He loves humanity and will go on loving;
   Over there are faith, life, virtue in the sun.

Index of First Lines

Pitch-dark night shuts in, and the rising gale, 78
Professing loud energy, out of the junction departed, 62

Round us the pines are darkness, 68

The Chinese tombs, 66
The gipsies lit their fires by the chalk-pit gate anew, 24
The haze upon the meadow, 36
The hop-poles stand in cones, 92
The old waggon drudges through the miry lane, 25
The time is gone when we could throw, 90
The train with its smoke and its rattle went on, 43
There the puddled lonely lane, 87
Though folks no more go Maying, 32
Tired with dull grief, grown old before my day, 59
Trenches in the moonlight, in the lulling moonlight, 61
Two buds we took from thousands more, 79

Under the thin green sky, the twilight day, 41
Up, my jewel! let's away, 84

Walking the river way to change our note, 38
We stood by the idle weir, 37
Whence is such glory? who would know, 39
Where tongues were loud and hearts were light, 57
With coat like any mole's, as soft and black, 26